Soul Training

Seven Keys to Coaching the Faith of Elite Sportspeople

Roger D. Lipe

Soul Training

Seven Keys to Coaching the Faith of Elite Sportspeople

Cross Training Publishing

www.crosstrainingpublishing.com

(308) 293-3891

Copyright © 2023 Roger D. Lipe

ISBN: 978-1-929478-23-1

The author acknowledges the valuable contributions of these people to this project:

- Coach Bryan Mullins for his suggestions.
- Rachel Aponte for her excellent work in graphic design, page layout, and formatting.
- Jenn Lipe for her editing and being an awesome daughter-in-law.
- Kathy Silvestri for the rear cover photo.

What people are saying about <u>Soul Training</u>:

"If you are serving high-profile athletes, coaches, or professionals in today's world, you must read <u>Soul Training</u>. Roger Lipe provides great insight on how to serve elite professionals, and people of sport."

Tommy Kyle
Executive Director - Nations of Coaches
Decatur, Alabama, United States of America

"As a historian, I study and write about many of the cultural and social factors that shape sports ministry. But getting to know Roger has reminded me of the beating heart that truly drives sports ministry: it's about relationships with people, time and presence.

Written with a spirit of generosity and service, this book provides a wealth of practical wisdom learned from a lifetime of experience. For chaplains and ministers working with athletes and coaches in elite sports, it is sure to be a helpful guide."

Paul Putz
Waco, Texas, USA

"I have known Roger for over a decade now, and what I love and admire about him and his work is that it's all about ensuring people become all that they are capable of becoming in every aspect of their life - body, mind and spirit. Roger knows the heart of God and he knows how athletes tick and speaks to the very heart of a person in such a practical and digestible way."

Warren H L Evans, MA
Chief Executive Officer
Sports Chaplaincy UK

"Roger and I have been friends for a long time, and I am grateful for his service to FCA and to the men and women of sport. His experience and his awareness of the heart of an athlete and coach make this book a must read. I am richer in spirit for having worked with him and learned from him over the years. The journey to know Jesus is fascinating. Taking along others that will help you in the race set before us is a must."

Rick Horton
Former MLB Pitcher
St. Louis Cardinals Broadcaster

"Simple and direct. Practical and actionable. Every sports chaplain new to the role is wise to learn from Roger's clear instruction, and veterans to the field will be challenged to humbly not forget their first love."

Marla Butterworth
FCA at 2007-2022 FCA staff at various universities.
2013-present Military Chaplaincy Reserves (USN and USAF).
2022-present FCA at US Air Force Academy - Colorado Springs, CO, USA

"I have read numerous books authored by Roger Lipe, but this is the most complete guide to developing, fostering, and growing a relationship with Jesus Christ through the experience of athletics. Roger has taken his years of experience and developed a laser focused strategy rooted in biblical truths and years of valuable experience. This is a homerun, a touchdown, and a buzzer-beating, game-winning three-pointer of a book!"

Coach Kerry Martin
Marion, IL USA

"I first met Roger in Hong Kong at the 2014 Asia Sports Chaplaincy Conference. In Asia we are always thankful of the faithfulness of Roger pouring out his life to represent Christ through Sports chaplaincy. This book Soul Training is once again going to be a blessing to the sports communities and beyond, reflecting the tenacity and rich wisdom on Roger's calling and experience for His Kingdom! It is indeed an elite soul training to the heart and equipped to impact communities. 100% recommended!!!"

Peter Jung
Director of Sports Chaplaincy Hong Kong

"This is a well-written and easy-to-understand treatise on the practical steps of ministering to people of sport. I don't think this is only for ministering to people of sport. The principles you document and write of so well can be helpful for ministers of the gospel in other areas. I have used your principles in reaching college students over the past few years and have found great success. These principles need to be taught, or should I say, caught by believers in the church. Your process of showing Christ to your athletes and coaches is encouraging."

Rev. Phillip W. Nelson
Pastor - Lakeland Baptist Church
Carbondale, Illinois

Introduction

This project is directed toward the Christian faith development of elite level competitors, their coaches, sports professionals, and high-profile people of sport. It is designed to be used by those coaches and competitors themselves, or by the leaders of sports ministries and local churches who serve them.

There are scores if not hundreds of books, discipleship guides, websites, and phone apps designed for the general public, but the people of sport we greatly respect and strongly love, are not like normal people.

Elite level sportspeople, their coaches, professional, and high-profile sportspeople are a miniscule fraction of the much larger set of millions of people who participate in sport for recreation, exercise, health benefits or social reasons. An exponentially greater number of people are those who consume sport as spectators. These elite sportspeople, in the USA mostly competing in collegiate sport, are fewer than four percent of those who compete in high school sports. Professional sportspeople are an even smaller percentage of those collegiate competitors, fewer than two percent of the elite men and women of sport.

Similar ratios between sports fans (greatest numbers), recreational sportspeople (fewer people), and elite sports people (very few people) are no doubt apparent in every nation of the world.

To be clear, anyone competing in college sport at any level in the USA is an elite level competitor. Anyone drawing a paycheck, of any size, for playing sport is a professional sportsperson. Anyone who coaches people at the elite or professional level is a sports professional. Any person of sport, regardless of age, who is widely recognizable beyond his family, teammates, and daily acquaintances, by a photo or one name only, is a high-profile sportsperson.

This chart, an adaptation of the principles found in the McCown Sport in Ministry Map, explained in great detail in Focus on Sport in Ministry by Lowrie McCown and Valerie Gin (ISBN - 193261100-2) contrasts the mindset and orientation toward sport between spectators, novices, and leisure-oriented sports participants, over against that of competitive, elite, and high-profile sportspeople.

Ministry Points of Emphasis from the McCown Sport in Ministry Map

Developed by Lowrie McCown

Elite and High-Profile Sportspeople	Spectators and Recreational Sportspeople
Identity Found in Sports Experience	Identity Found Outside Sports Experience
Relational approach	Programmatic approach
High Achievement Sport	Recreational Sport
Values Performance	Values Winning
Processes	Results
Discuss Sports Experience	Share Sports Testimonies
Ask Questions	Make Statements
Specialized Appeal	Mass Appeal
Complex	Simple

Sports ministry leaders are often a little puzzled as they encounter elite and professional sportspeople. They expect them to be just like other people, but their lives in sport often present obstacles to their involvement in church services and ministry events that are a great fit for the general population.

I have been serving coaches and student-athletes at Southern Illinois University in Carbondale, for nearly thirty years, as well as eight years with a professional baseball club, and in that time I have learned several factors that are key to effectively engaging, serving, building relationships with, and making disciples among the coaches and players in our community. I hope these simple thoughts serve you and your ministry well.

The following is a quick overview of those factors:

- Respect their time constraints.
- Embrace their sport's culture.
- Communicate directly.
- Demonstrate genuine interest in them.

- Invite them into your home.
- Love extravagantly.
- Serve selflessly.

In addition to the expansion of each of these factors will be illustrative narratives for each, a final section with faith development exercises that have proven effective across many decades, as well as occasional notes of emphasis for service in professional sport from a forerunner for many of us, the late Walt Enoch of the Fellowship of Christian Athletes in St. Louis, Missouri.

The general outline for this project was excerpted from an article titled <u>Six Keys to Discipling Student-Athletes</u>, which I wrote for <u>Collegiate Collective</u> in September of 2015 (http://collegiatecollective.com/6-keys-discipling-student-athletes/#.Y4KYg3bMK5e)

Portions of this project are excerpted from the blog - https://sportchaplainsportmentor.blogspot.com by Roger D. Lipe.

Points of Emphasis for Professional Sport (As outlined by Walt Enoch)

Walt Enoch began serving professional athletes in 1970 when only the Los Angeles Dodgers and Chicago Cubs had chapel leaders. He was already serving the St. Louis Cardinals when Baseball Chapel began its ministry. Walt also served the St. Louis Football Cardinals before they moved to Arizona and served the St. Louis Rams. For two years he had a ministry with the NHL's St. Louis Blues. For many years he worked to oversee all the baseball chapel leaders in the Cardinals' minor league cities.

Among Walt's core values for serving in this role are:

- Love
- Service
- Acceptance of others (teach it to them)
- Christ-centered ministry

Respect their time constraints.

Wendy (Goodman) Bauersachs is my friend. She is a 6'-2" (1.88 meters) beautiful young lady, daughter, sister, friend, and teammate. She is now a wife, the mother of three, teaches second grade, and coaches junior high basketball. She was also #44 for Saluki Women's Basketball (Southern Illinois University – USA).

A few weeks after the end of her playing career, she called me asking, "Rog, what do normal people do with all this time?" She had encountered the sense of lost identity that most sportspeople experience at the end of their sporting careers. After going to the gym for practice most every day since she was twelve-years-of-age, now she had no more practice, no more games, no more team, or teammates, or coaches. She suddenly used to be a basketball player.

Every competitor, regardless of talent, level of competition, length of professional contract, or wealth accumulated, at some point experiences the end of their career and deals with the change in lifestyle including the unexpected abundance of time on their hands. Just like Wendy.

Being a collegiate athlete is like going to school full-time and working a full-time job, at the same time. They have practice six days a week, they often spend extra hours in voluntary work on the mental part of the game, they must study just like any student, and they want to have a social life like any other student. Add on in-season travel, injury rehabilitation, off-season workouts, and mandatory community service projects, and their lives are crowded and complex.

The lifestyle of collegiate coaches is even more consuming as they have each logged hours of watching game video, building game plans, staff meetings, position meetings, personal video review with players, and more before they ever get to practice with their players. All that is in addition to the hours of video review, travel, visits with, and evaluation of recruits for their next class of players.

For the coaches and competitors in professional sport, it is much the same. They just don't have to go to class. Now their lives in sport are even more consuming with countless hours of time in the office, at training, and in practice. Sadly, many of these coaches spend the night sleeping in their offices rather than going home.

The ministry point here is to respect the value of free time. When we do events, I limit them to one hour. If athletes want to hang around longer, good, but if they need to get in and out, they are free. Be sure to ask lots of questions about their schedules and design your activities for them to fit their best days and hours.

Consider the schedule described in the article excerpt below, <u>Flaws of the Twenty Hour Rule</u>, by Katie Lever, M.A. and posted in 2adays.com.

Every prospective athlete understands that life as a college athlete is time-consuming. I remember during my time in the NCAA, telling recruits that they would have to learn time management skills once they started competing, which, while not technically untrue, was the understatement of the century. A teammate of mine used to tell recruits about the college athlete triangle: "As a college athlete, you want three things: good grades and athletic performances, a social life, and sleep. You can only pick two."

My teammate was dead-on. Time works differently for college athletes, no thanks to the so-called limitations the NCAA places on practice and competition time. These measures are detailed in the 2019-2020 version of the Division I Manual under Bylaw 17.1.7.1, which states: "A student-athlete's participation in countable athletically related activities shall be limited to a maximum of four hours per day and 20 hours per week."

Before I get into the shortfalls of the 20-hour rule, we need to rewind to Bylaw 17.02.14, which lists required athletically related activities, defined as "any activities, including those that are countable in the daily and weekly limitations, that are required of a student-athlete." These activities are not considered countable toward the NCAA's 20-hour limit (the NCAA published a chart that illustrates the differences between countable/noncountable time), and the manual then provides a non-exhaustive list of required (but non-countable) activities:

- Compliance meetings
- Organized team promotional activities
- Recruiting activities, including student-host duties
- Media activities
- Fundraising events
- Community service events
- Team-building activities
- Travel to and from away-from-home competition

In short, activities such as scheduled practices, competition days, and film sessions are considered countable, while the activities listed above are not. The NCAA requires coaches to give athletes at least one day off per week (which athletes are not required to take—they can still work out if the workout is considered voluntary). Travel days can also count as days off (for nonautonomy schools), if no mandatory countable athletically related activities take place that day, or 24 hours following a return trip that takes place between midnight and 5:00 AM.

Confused? That's understandable. To clear things up, here's a glimpse of an itinerary from my sophomore year as a distance runner at Western Kentucky University covering a four-day track trip from WKU to Stanford University. This time around, I played coach and logged the hours. Here are my calculations, following the NCAA's time limit guidelines for nonautonomy schools:

Day 1 (Wednesday)

5:00-6:00 AM CST: Wake up/ "voluntary" shakeout run (0 hr. of countable athletically-related time)

6:00-7:00 AM CST: Shower/breakfast, walk to stadium to find team vans

7:00-8:00 AM CST: Drive to Nashville airport (0 hrs. of countable athletically-related time)

10:00 AM CST-3:00 PM PST: Fly to San Francisco (0 hrs. of countable athletically-related time)

3:00-4:00 PM PST: Drive from airport to hotel (0 hrs. of countable athletically-related time)

5:00-9:00 PM PST: Dinner/downtime/bed.

Total countable athletically-related time: 0 hours

Actual time spent traveling/competing: 9 hours

*If, as a coach, I deem an athlete's workout "voluntary," this travel day could also be considered a day off, according to Bylaw 17.1.7.4.1, which states "A travel day related to athletics participation may be considered as a day off, provided no countable athletically related activities occur during that day." Hence, day one could potentially count as zero hours toward the 20-hour limit. Even if my run was mandatory, at most, day one would only be countable as one hour of countable time, since travel to and from competition doesn't count.

Day 2 (Thursday)

8:00-9:00 AM PST: Shakeout run (1 hr. of countable athletically-related time)

9:00AM-12:00PM PST: Shower/breakfast/study time

12:00-5:00PM: Lunch/sightseeing

6:00PM-7:00PM: Dinner

7:30-10:00PM: Study time/bed

Total countable athletically-related time: 1 hour

Actual time spent traveling/competing: 1 hour

Day 3 (Competition Friday)

9:00-9:30 AM PST: Shakeout run (0.5 hr. countable athletically-related time)

9:30AM-6:00PM: Shower, meals, study, race prep

6:00-6:30: Drive to track (0.5 hr. countable athletically-related time)

7:00-9:00 PM PST: warm-up/ 10k race/cool down (2 hrs countable athletically-related time)

9:30-10:00PM PST: drive back to hotel (0.5 hrs countable athletically-related time)

11:00: bed

Total countable athletically-related time: 3 hours*

Actual time spent traveling/competing: 3.5 hours

*Here is another tricky element of the 20-hour rule, outlined in Bylaw 17.1.7.3.2, which states "All competition and any associated athletically related activities on the day of competition shall count as three hours regardless of the actual duration of these activities." That knocks 30 minutes off the countable athletically-related time for this day.

Day 4/5 (Saturday & Sunday)

7:00-8:00 AM PST: Shakeout run (1 hr. countable athletically-related time)

8:00-11:00 AM PST: Shower/breakfast/pack/study

11:00-12:00 AM PST: Drive to airport (0 hrs. countable athletically-related time)

2:00 PM PST-10:00 PM CST: Fly back to Nashville (0 hrs. countable athletically-related time)

11:00 PM CST- 12:00 AM CST: Drive home from airport (0 hr. countable athletically-related time)

1:00 AM CST: Bed

Total countable athletically-related time: 1 hour

Actual time spent traveling/competing: 9 hours

Here are the grand totals for my four-day trip

Total countable athletically-related time for the entire trip: 5 hours

Actual time spent travelling/competing: 22.5 hours

As you can see, I ran (no pun intended) 2.5 hours over the NCAA's 20-hour cap over the span of four days, not seven, but the trip only counted as 5 hours.

* Originally published on August 31, 2021, by Katie Lever, M.A. https://www.2adays.com/blog/flaws-of-the-20-hour-rule/

Embrace their sport's culture.

Several years ago, I invited a series of local pastors to address our college (American) football team during pregame chapels. I chose these pastors carefully, seeking men who could deliver well on a talk, and pastors whose churches I could heartily recommend our players attend.

One Saturday morning, I was very confident of the pastor and his impending talk because a number of our players and hundreds of other college students attended his church. I knew him to be a guy who worked out regularly, and he was significantly younger than I was.

As soon as he arrived in the room for chapel and the pregame meal, I knew we were in trouble. The pregame meal is just four hours prior to game time, and both coaches and players are never more focused than they are in this hour. I welcomed the pastor to my table, and as he sat down, he said, "Wow, it's pretty intense in here, isn't it?" I said, "Yeah, isn't it awesome?" The pastor was terribly intimidated by the intensity of the environment. I said, "Hey, you need to get your stuff together because you'll be up in a couple of minutes."

After receiving the queue from the Head Coach to begin chapel, I had a player open with a prayer and introduced the pastor. His first words were, "It's really intense in here, and I'm a little intimidated." It went downhill from there. After he finished, I tried to recover the moment and to help us prepare to compete.

The problem was obvious to everyone but the pastor. He neither understood nor respected the culture of college football. He certainly did not grasp why these people in this moment would be so intensely focused. We're still friends, but I never asked him to address the team again.

Too often, we in the Church tolerate sport culture and try to relate to elite, professional, and high-profile sportspeople while firmly entrenched in church culture. Sportspeople are not against church culture; they just don't understand it.

They have lived in and are deeply immersed in their unique sport's culture. Too many of my sport chaplain and character coach colleagues endure the culture of sport while anxious to get to their opportunity to speak. Competitors and coaches feel the distance and are hesitant to respond to those of such an attitude.

The way to break through this issue is to heartily embrace the sport culture, warts and all, and thereby communicate unconditional acceptance to those who live therein. Beware the temptation to simply add sports clichés to your vocabulary. Poorly applied sports language raises the red flags of "phony," "poser," and "wannabe." As we learn to speak their language, to fit into their schedules, and to understand their values, we are more able to serve and to speak effectively.

How comfortably do you live in the culture of your sport? Does it fit like a well-worn batting glove or more like a size eight shoe on your size twelve foot? Do you find it relaxing or stressful? Do you speak its language and enjoy its nuances of gesture and posture or do you seem like an outsider? As you serve Christ in the world of sport, do you live in its culture and work to transform it or simply import Church culture into sport?

Can you speak the language of baseball with baseball players, or do you speak churchy language in the dugout? Do you find yourself at ease in the culture of football or do the footballers look at you like you don't belong on the pitch? Does the practice gym and all its sounds and smells seem pleasant to you or do they itch your soul like a bad sweater?

To import church culture into the sport world is simpler, less costly and far less effective. It's easy to speak to players and coaches in the cloistered language of the Church, but it's really hard to communicate deeply that way. It's simple to tell stories about church leaders from the 18th century or the high-profile player you saw on television last weekend, but it's much harder to listen intently and to watch closely the life of your team so as to speak their language and engage their hearts. It's quick, painless, and trouble-free to tolerate the culture of sport in order to find a moment in which you can cram your canned presentation. It's much less effective than building the relationships which allow you to speak clearly to the hearts of those who trust you.

To live in the sport culture is to wear its kit, to speak its language, to read its periodicals, books, journals and to listen to its prophets. The prophets of sport culture are most found in the newspapers, talk radio, sports magazines, on blogs or web sites. Can you hear them? Will you take the time to wrestle with the issues of daily life in sport? Do you have an answer to their questions? To live in the sport culture is to know its history, to respect its leaders and to relax in its sounds, sights, smells and emotions.

To be an agent of Christ's transforming power in sport culture is to demonstrate God-honoring values and to love people extravagantly in the daily life of sport. It's simply insufficient to tell Sunday School stories, to repeat tired clichés and to recycle last month's sermon for this week's chapel talk. If we speak of worship being something that happens exclusively within the walls of the church and exclude the activity of sport as an expression of genuine worship and praise to God, we miss our opportunity to help sports people experience real joy and fulfillment.

I would challenge you to do the same as many missionary leaders of past centuries and to take off the ill-fitting cultural trappings of the Church which only confuse and often repel those you seek to serve. Then begin to live in the culture of the sport in which you serve while striving to communicate the love of God in relevant terms. Above all, put on the character of Christ Jesus. Such character is broader than any culture, adapts well to any situation, and transforms hearts and minds by the application of Truth and extravagant love.

Points of Emphasis for Professional Sport (As outlined by Walt Enoch)

- In NFL Football – the team chaplain serves at the pleasure of the Head Coach. That relationship is most important. Walt says, "He runs the machine. I'm just a spark plug."

- He makes it a point to introduce and offer service to all in the organization, trainers, doctors, office personnel, etc.
- With NFL players, Walt recognizes that the pro football player comes from a college atmosphere where he is considered very highly, often leading to an air of entitlement in the player. Don't be put off by it, but understand who they are.
- In Major League Baseball (MLB) – Baseball Chapel appoints the chapel leaders and works through an application and interview process.
- The Baseball Chapel leader mostly relates to the players. Seldom do coaches, managers or support personnel participate in chapels.
- With MLB players, Walt recognizes that these players come up through the minor league system with very little money and a tough road to reach the major leagues. Because of this arduous process, there is much less of a sense of entitlement among them.
- One should not expect a strong sense of community among professional sports teammates off the field of competition. Once out the locker room or clubhouse, it's seldom that they spend a lot of time with their teammates.
- As one is building his relationship with players, it's important to not be seen as a part of the club's organization. If one is too closely tied to the management, it could compromise his trust among the players.
- I asked Walt about how to handle transitions for players and coaches (trades, free agency, waivers, firings, etc.), and he said that if your relationship is strong, one should call the player or coach as soon as possible. Arrange to meet with the player or coach. Encourage, counsel, console, and work to maintain the relationship if possible. Though it's difficult, some relationships have been able to last for many years beyond the player's career in sport.
- Walt made a point to not forget the players when their playing careers are over. He arranged a separate Bible study for former players. (It's best not to mix current and former players. It's awkward for both sets of people.)

Communicate directly.

Just before to the start of a November 2008 pre-game chapel, a (American) football player stopped by my table and said that he'd like to talk with me. I said we would talk after the pregame meal. As most of the room had cleared, I walked to his table and asked him what I could do for him. He began to tell me of the five years of regret he has suffered because he didn't tell his grandmother that he loved her prior to her untimely death in their home on this very day.

Tears were running down his face as he told the story. It seems his every waking moment was haunted by these five years of regret and the only free moments he had were as he played football, as it required his full attention. He was feeling pressure because he knew he was running out of football games. I assured him of his grandmother's love and respect, and we talked about how to move this grieving process along. We talked about some short-term things to do today and a few more to do in the coming days and weeks. I prayed with him at the table and then turned him loose.

After leaving the dining room, I walked to the stadium to pray for the players and coaches. As I walked up and down the field, I prayed for each unit of the team and their responsibilities as well as for the coaching staff. As I was praying and walking, I could see my grieving friend sitting quietly at the top of the stadium, and I knew he was doing one of the things I had suggested just minutes ago. I was praying that his heart would be free to compete at his best and to release the regret that had plagued him for years. As I was leaving the stadium, I met him at the gate, and I spoke with him, and he said he felt great.

The player's sanctuary of freedom and relaxation was faithful to him again, but today he played with even greater liberty due to having dealt with his painful regret. He played his heart out and rushed for two-hundred-fifty-six yards and two touchdowns on the day. More than any achievement on the field that day, he had broken through five years of torment and sorrow into freedom and confidence. Now he can feel free and forgiven on and off the field.

Shortly thereafter this player made a commitment to Christ at a local church and was baptized a week later. I believe the release of his five years of regret and self-imposed guilt had truly freed his heart to trust Christ Jesus for all his life. The opportunity for clear, direct communication about matters of the heart, and the player's vulnerability were built on trust won across two years. To communicate directly fit the culture of college football and the urgency of the moment.

Occasionally I will invite a local pastor to address our team in a pregame chapel. I give them a time frame to fit, a general idea of theme or topic, answer their questions, and then turn them loose. That usually goes fairly well, but occasionally it does not. The errors are usually a matter of not fitting sport culture or a clumsy importation of church culture into the sport setting. Sport is a culture of direct language. Time is always at a premium. Communication is always straight forward. There is no room for dropping hints, for being subtle, or for being overly artful in one's speech. There is no need for elaborate introductions, for jokes, or for allegory. Speak directly with coaches and competitors. Get to the point. Ask direct questions. They will not take offense or find you pushy.

Below are a couple of email responses I sent to a veteran college baseball coach, in a battle with cancer, when he asked me, "Does the Bible have anything to say about failure?"

"Coach, I've been thinking through the issue of failure and the Biblical examples of it, they're all over the place.

- Moses failed by committing murder and was exiled for forty years but came back to Egypt and was used of God in a powerful way.
- David, the king, failed by committing adultery with Bathsheba and conspiring to have her husband killed but was restored and was used of God in a powerful way.
- Peter, the apostle, failed by denying that he knew Jesus three times but was used of God in a powerful way.
- Judas failed by betraying Jesus for thirty pieces of silver and hung himself in despair.

- Three were utter failures who were restored and one failure who lost all hope and was destroyed.

These were Jesus' words to Peter, even before he was to fail later that same night, *'Simon, stay on your toes. Satan has tried his best to separate all of you from me, like chaff from wheat. Simon, I've prayed for you in particular that you do not give in or give out. When you have come through the time of testing, turn to your companions, and give them a fresh start.'*

The point seems to be that failure is the human condition, but that we can press through it, we can be restored and emerge better than we were before the failure. That has certainly been my experience through all my years. I have failed plenty, but I trust God to make me better through the experience.

Baseball is built on failure and recovery. A hitter goes to the hall of fame if he fails 2/3 of the time. Hitting is one player vs. nine, a perfect design for failure. It takes four balls to walk, but only three strikes for an out. Just throwing strikes is terribly challenging for pitchers.

It seems that the ones who deal best with failure are the ones who don't treat it as an enemy but as an ally. They strongly pursue success and excellence but know that short-term failure is inevitable, and they learn from it and improve. The batter who strikes out his first three at bats can come up in his fourth and get the game winning hit. Suddenly successful amid failure."

Coach's reply: "Thank you so much, Roger. I have read this, and I am going to save it and reread it on occasion. I have to remind myself that failure in baseball is inevitable. I just do not like it, and because of that, I take the losses way too personally and way harder than I accept the wins. Thanks for caring."

My reply: "Sadly, failure is not only a part of baseball but life in general. I also take losses in sport personally and feel them at the heart. To do otherwise feels like betrayal to me. I feel I owe it to my teammates to care deeply and to feel the sting of loss as acutely as I feel the exhilaration of victory.

I believe that's a part of what Christ Jesus has done for us, to give us hope beyond the failure and to fuel our hearts for competing our hearts out again in the next game, the next day, the next treatment.

Let's both commit ourselves to pressing through life's failures to experience Christ's gift of hope and faith."

Summary: I believe the Lord uses such communication, simple and direct, in a similar way to the way He uses epistles in the New Testament. Paul wrote to his disciples and churches he had founded very directly, whereas he was much gentler when face to face. Let's prayerfully consider the power of the written word to communicate God's heart for the people of sport, and then we can follow up those words with face to face, compassionate and caring relationship building.

One of the keys to effective communication with people of sport is clear and direct language. There is no need, nor time for frills, skillfully crafted rhetoric, or subtleties of speech. Write and speak directly to be understood, to inspire, to challenge, and to call to action. Such language fits the sporting culture and carries the message of Christ's love and care very well.

Demonstrate genuine interest.

What can we learn from a tattoo? What is to be learned from the ink painfully pressed beneath a person's skin? Tattoos are seldom either profound works of literature or wondrous works of art. They do, however, give us a glimpse at the heart which is expressing itself through his or her skin.

The world of sport is rife with tattooed men and women. From the high-profile sportspeople to the most obscure high school student-athlete with a hunger to honor a fallen teammate, tattoos are very prevalent in this culture. Many who follow Christ are quick to make judgments about tattoos and their propriety for other followers of Jesus. It is not my intention to make judgments either way, but to consider what a person is telling us from his or her choice of tattoo and the possibility that well worded questions about them can open a pathway to heart-felt discussions about the real matters of life.

In team-building sessions with a USA university men's basketball and American football teams, I have used questions like these for discussion among the players in small groups and then with the team at large. "If you have a tattoo, tell us about it. What does it represent? When did you get it? Do you have any regrets about having it now?" The responses to these thoughts were varied and remarkable. One player said, "I do not have any tattoos. It would displease my parents, and I will not do anything to disrespect my parents." I was stunned. Another player, with over twenty tattoos, said, "My left arm is dedicated to my mother. My right arm is dedicated to my grade school classmate who died when we were eleven years old. My chest and back speak of things which are important to me." More than I expected said that they had no tattoos, and not even one would say he regretted having it, a strong contrast to many men of my generation who wish the US Marine Corps bulldog on their shoulders or the US Navy anchors on their forearms were no longer there. This lack of regret may simply be a function of age.

Just among athletes, I have seen tattoos on feet, ankles, shins, calves, thighs, lower backs, upper backs, torsos, upper chests, shoulders, biceps, forearms, whole sleeves of tattoos, tattoos on fingers, on necks and even under one's hair. My daughter-in-law, a track athlete, has the word, "Strength" on the top of her foot. A friend who was a USA high jumper in the 1996 Olympics has the Olympic rings above his ankle. Without exception, there is a reason for what is written or drawn. The bearer of the tattoo is expressing his heart through the ink. Their hearts are sometimes foolish, sometimes they were received in the fog of an alcohol or drug infused mind, but in all cases the tattoo means something.

Getting to the something, discerning the meaning and the athlete's heart is what I am asking you to consider. Starting the discussion is often as simple as asking a question like the one listed earlier. I have asked that question in formal settings like Team Building sessions, while standing beside a basketball court while players drank water, while standing on the sideline at football practice and while sitting together over coffee. In every case, I hear layers of answers. There is usually the surface level "public answer" which satisfies most people, but I am looking for something more. There must be something deeper here to justify the pain, time and cash invested in the ink below one's skin. Asking follow up questions which enable one to share a story about the acquisition of the tattoo, the circumstances surrounding it and the significance of the word, or the symbol can help us hear their hearts and can open a path to speak to their hearts most directly. Be careful, you may not want to hear some of what you're told.

Demonstrate genuine interest in the people of sport, not just in the results of their competitions. For far too long the Church has been pleased to "use" sportspeople for their ministry ends and to trade on their celebrity status for institutional gain. Such a utilitarian attitude leads many student-athletes to keep the Church at arm's length.

When our first interaction with a coach or competitor is to ask about the results of their most recent contest, their defenses go up immediately, especially if the results were less than good. To only ask about results or prospects for upcoming games is to diminish them as people. Ask questions about family, school, practice and teammates, or anything related to the process of being an elite or professional sportsperson. This demonstrates an understanding that he or she is more than an animal in a uniform.

Love the coach or competitor, not his or her celebrity status in the community.

Demonstrate genuine interest in sportspeople by asking questions to draw them into conversation and then to probe more deeply toward their hearts.

Three levels of questions:

1.   Questions that solicit facts. I ask the competitor's name, hometown, position, uniform number, etc. These are mostly facts. Most anyone will offer these details.

2.   Questions that elicit passion. I ask about the competitor's sporting experiences, and I'm looking for their love for the sport. I am leading them to tell me stories that awaken their passion for sport, team, competition, coaches, etc.

3.   Questions that solicit their hearts. I ask about the matters at the core of who they are: values, faith, relationships, events, and other factors that shape their lives from the very center.

Please consider this brief list as a place to start with those whom you serve. Always ask process questions, not results questions. Fans and media only ask questions about results.

1. How is your team developing? Is the teamwork good?

2. How pleased are you with your _____? (training, practice, hitting, rehab, etc.)

3. How pleased are you with preparations for your next competition?

4. Who among your teammates is doing very well?

5. What are some challenges you have encountered?

6. What sorts of situations in your sport bring out the best of your abilities?

7. How well is your team connecting with the coaching staff?

8. When your playing days are over, what do you think you will miss most about sport?

9. What are the situations in your sport that are most difficult for you?

10. Who are your most trusted teammates?

11. When and where are you most fully the person you want to be?

12. What elements of your life in sport are most pleasing to you?

13. What is there about your life in sport that will still be important to you 10 years from now?

14. When you are on the _____ (floor, field, court, track, mat, pitch, etc..), do you feel that God is near or distant? Engaged or disinterested? Pleased or disgusted? Why?

Points of Emphasis for Professional Sport (as outlined by Walt Enoch)

With professional sportspeople, serving their spouses and children is an important part of effective ministry. Often, it's the most mundane tasks which win the chaplain favor and trust with the family and consequently, the player or coach.

- Driving family members to the airport to drop off or pick someone up.
- Helping families move into their new home or to move out when traded, fired or waived.
- Helping families find real estate agents, schools, day care, family doctors, churches, etc.

We discussed the high-profile nature of many players and how to deal with those who fail publicly, especially moral failure. How should the chaplain handle those situations?

- Love them.
- Seek them out.
- Don't confront their behavior, rather be available to them and when they open the subject, be clear, loving, and direct.

Invite them into your home.

For many years my wife and I have been privileged to host groups of coaches, elite athletes (from athletics, volleyball, basketball, swimming and diving, American football, baseball, softball, golf, football [soccer], and tennis), and professional baseball players in our home for meetings and meals.

At the beginning of each new semester, I would ask the college athletes where they would like to hold the upcoming series of meetings, and every time they would say, "Let's meet at your house." I would ask them why, and they would reply, "It's peaceful." I came to understand that simply means it's not like a dorm room or a noisy apartment building. It could also have to do with the delicious snacks my wife would prepare for each week's meeting.

For years we have been inviting coaching staffs to our home for a big breakfast on a workday morning following the preseason preparations and just prior to the first game of the season. This simple, one-hour meal together works wonders in building relationships of trust and commitment. There is something special about having this group in our home that cannot be duplicated in a restaurant, coffee shop, or staff meeting room.

During one summer evening's dinner with an entire college (American) football team, hosted in our modest apartment, among the dozens of players from all across the country who were consuming a mountain of tacos was a freshman whose language included a string of profanities in a single sentence. One of his elder teammates stopped him abruptly and said, "Hey, we don't talk like that in this house." This veteran player's love and respect for my wife led him to correct his rookie teammate. I was gratified by his expression of respect for our hospitality and our values for life.

Without question, some of the most deeply impactful moments of making disciples and building depth of relationship have occurred in my home. As we have welcomed coaches and competitors into our home for studies, for meals, for picnics, coffee, or discussions, they find our place to be peaceful and like home.

Your home does not feel like a dorm room, a noisy apartment, an office, or even the chaotic homes from where many have come. Be mindful that you may be their model for what a Christ-honoring marriage looks like. (77% of college basketball players in the USA come from one or zero parent homes.) Yours may be the only healthy home life they have ever seen. How you live in front of them can be transformational, all by itself.

Consider any or all these opportunities for hospitality with the elite sportspeople in your community:

- Breakfast in your home with the coaching staff.
- An off-season cookout with the team.
- A regular discussion in your kitchen over coffee.
- Host a Bible study and provide a simple snack.
- Prepare a lunch or dinner and take it to the coaches' offices during their most time-consuming days.

One of the best days of my life in serving sportspeople happened in my home over a breakfast casserole with two young coaches. Both young men were in our FCA campus ministry at Southern Illinois University, one was a baseball player and the other played American football. Both were now coaching high school sports, one softball and the other football. I had given them each a copy of Coach Joe Ehrmann's book, InsideOutCoaching. (ISBN – 1439182981) They each sought me out saying, "We like the ideas in this book, but we have to figure out how to do it." I said, "How about next Saturday morning, you two come to our house, we'll have a great breakfast together, and we'll discuss how to put these ideas into practice?" We agreed and talked for three hours over a hearty breakfast and lots of coffee. It is an enduring joy to know that morning's conversation was a part of the preparation process for two of the most transformational coaches I know anywhere in the world.

Points of Emphasis for Professional Sport (As outlined by Walt Enoch)

Walt and his wife have found that holidays (Easter, Thanksgiving, Christmas, and others) were outstanding opportunities to serve players' and coaches' families through hospitality. Having them in their home made a real impact with the players, coaches, and their families.

Love extravagantly.

Most every day of my life of service with the people of sport has included at least one encounter that either grieved my soul or annoyed my flesh. Many times, both occurred in the same moment. Having grown up in church and never learning how to curse, it's easy to become offended at coarse language and to project a self-righteous attitude. A dose of self-awareness and a brief look in the mirror at my sarcastic tongue is all it takes to overcome such attitudes.

Having served Women's Basketball teams for twenty-eight years, I have had great relationships with many players and coaches who were in same-sex relationships. The openness and genuine love we experienced was rather perplexing to many of my friends in the Church, and frankly, to many of my sports ministry colleagues.

I have had numerous conversations with coaches and competitors who shared, sometimes in vivid detail, stories of their sexual exploits. I watched their expressions as they would look to see if I would criticize, condemn, or be dismissive of them. My own lustful heart and my soul's awareness of it kept me from shaming them or pronouncing condemnation.

I have read II Corinthians 5:16-17 for many years, having committed verse 17 to memory years ago. More recently, I began focusing on verse 16, ***Therefore from now on we recognize no one according to the flesh; even though we have known Christ according to the flesh, yet now we know Him in this way no longer.*** (NASB) I have paraphrased the first half of that verse to say, "Therefore from now on we will not allow anyone's flesh (sin) to be his or her defining characteristic." This text revolutionized my approach to people who sin differently from me, and it allowed me to appropriate Jesus' extravagant love to them.

I refuse to see a coach approaching me and think, "Here comes Coach Lesbian." I will not see a player and immediately think, "He's a rotten womanizer." My soul will no longer allow me to think of a coach as, "the drunken fool." Christ's extravagant love, irresistible grace, and abundant mercy demands that I no longer allow anyone's flesh to be his or her defining characteristic. I choose to see the person as one for whom Christ died, and to whom I am called to love and serve. This conviction has revolutionized my service of the people of sport.

People of sport are often less than loveable. Much of the life of a coach, elite or professional athlete is less than lovely. Ministry with them often smells bad and sounds coarse. It requires extravagant love. It is not safe, is seldom convenient, and is certainly not normal. It is, however, extremely rewarding.

When one invests deeply, loves powerfully, and pays the price to care for the competitors and coaches, they respond in faith with the same passion they bring to sport. It is dynamic and worth every moment.

One of the values held in highest regard in United States culture is "tolerance." We are implored from every angle, in the media and in schools, that we must tolerate everything and everyone around us. This value is extolled as the highest form of human virtue and should be applied to not only ethnic and religious differences, but to every form of behavior and even to those engaged in foolish, abusive or self-abusing lifestyles. I beg to differ. Tolerance is simply too benign, too soft, too passive to be reflective of Christ Jesus' Church. I believe He wants more from us than benign tolerance; He wants us to love people extravagantly. We who serve the men and women of sport are surrounded by many who are easy to love and others which we find at least distasteful and maybe even repulsive.

Here are some simple thoughts which contrast extravagant love and benign tolerance:

- Extravagant love takes risks for people. Benign tolerance is safe and secure as it keeps people at a distance.
- Extravagant love embraces people and their imperfections. Benign tolerance puts up with people we find distasteful or odd.
- Extravagant love is very costly as it pays the price to seek others' best. Benign tolerance is cheap and requires little of the one tolerating the others.

- Extravagant love is active and seeks out those whom we love. Benign tolerance is passive and feels relieved when those tolerated are not around.

- Extravagant love expects the best from others and hopes persistently. Benign tolerance expects little from others and simply hopes to not be disappointed.

- Extravagant love invests deeply in others. Benign tolerance invests shallowly, sharing only what is required.

- Extravagant love honors Christ as it directly reflects His nature. Benign tolerance honors no one as it is purely self-centered and self-protecting, honoring neither the tolerant or the tolerated.

The obvious problem for all of us is that some people really annoy us. Some people's habits, lifestyles, behavior, or cultural trappings may tear at the very fabric of our convictions and make our flesh scream for relief and distance from these people. Tolerance offers you a low-cost, risk-free solution to your dilemma. It is, however, not worthy of our Lord. Extravagant love is what our Lord modeled for us and has even empowered us to demonstrate. His grace is given to each of us in sufficient measure to love even the most repulsive people in our circles of relationships.

My challenge to you is to press through the easy, cheap, secure, low expectations of tolerance and take the risk, pay the cost, actively and deeply, even extravagantly love the people around you. Coaches, competitors, physios, equipment managers, club officials, athletic directors, support staff, the foolish, the perverse, the profane, the abusive, the rebellious, all of them. Jesus' blood was shed for each of them and His grace, in you, is sufficient to enable you to love them beyond your wildest imaginations.

Serve selflessly.

Across several seasons of college (American) football, the head coaches asked me to help with the development of the team's leadership group. That was usually between 6 and 12 young men, and we would meet weekly to discuss a leadership development item I would have prepared to share with them. In addition, we would assign and review a few leadership exercises they would execute. These were often simply saying, "thank you," to members of the support staff, writing cards of appreciation to people surrounding the program, and responsibilities for the condition of locker rooms, buses, and airplanes.

I would ask for two volunteers each to oversee the cleaning of the locker room on game day, as well as for the buses or airplane upon our arrival home. I was also with them to help oversee the process.

As soon as the game was over, we had prayed together, and the head coach had made his postgame remarks, we began the process of getting out of uniform, cutting off tape, showering, gathering up uniforms, and bagging shoes, shoulder pads, helmets, and other pads. To clean the locker room to our standard meant lots of hands picking up discarded tape, towels, and other debris. It also meant carrying about eighty heavy bags full of gear out to the truck for the drive home.

The team leaders and their sixty-plus-year-old team chaplain would each have a pair of equipment bags in each hand, carrying them to the truck. Neither they nor I had to do this, but it was important to model for the leaders and they for their teammates, what selfless service looks like. It would have been much easier to simply hop on the bus and to consume the postgame dinner. This expression of service was of great value to everyone involved, even the old man.

Whereas elite and professional sportspeople and coaches grow accustomed to people asking them to do things, we must be the ones to serve them with no thought of receiving anything in return. They find this both refreshing and endearing. This builds trust. This opens hearts.

To perform the most menial tasks with and for them is a profound relationship builder. Serve without fanfare. Don't take selfies with them and post them online. Don't ask for autographs, free tickets, or sideline privileges. Such presumption is the essence of selfishness, and they find it repulsive. Give yourself away in helping them, and you will find a loyal friend and an inquisitive heart.

Ministry to sportspeople is selflessly serving them and God's purposes in them with no ulterior motive.

Below are some examples of such selfless service -

- Assisting in the whole-life development of the sportsperson.
- Offering help to competitors' and coaches' families when they are new to the community.
- Assisting support staff when they need help with a task.
- Visiting competitors who are injured, ill, or are grieving a family loss.
- Helping a coach or competitor who wants to share his faith by training and encouraging him in it.
- Offering hospitality and community to these people often displaced from family and friends.
- Speaking privately with a competitor or coach about his or her relationship with Christ.
- Maintaining confidentiality re: injuries, illness, family situations, contracts, etc.
- Protecting private information about competitors and coaches, such as phone numbers, email addresses, etc.
- Praying for a coach or competitor when a request is shared in confidence.
- Sending encouraging notes, text messages, and phone calls.

Points of Emphasis for Professional Sport (As outlined by Walt Enoch)

With professional sportspeople, serving their spouses and children is an important part of effective ministry. Many times, it's the most mundane tasks which win the chaplain favor and trust with the family and consequently, the player or coach.

- Driving family members to the airport to drop off or pick someone up.
- Helping families move into their new home or to move out when traded, fired or waived.
- Helping families find real estate agents, schools, day care, family doctors, churches, etc.

Walt made it a point to introduce and offer service to all in the organization: trainers, doctors, office personnel, etc.

Because the chaplain is given entrance to places most people cannot go and thereby comes by information that most people don't have, I asked Walt about how to handle this privilege. His answers follow:

- Moments of crisis are particularly important for the chaplain to be available to the team or individuals. He mentioned the in-season death of a player and the respect that he was shown by the club as they flew him to be with the team.

Teach, Mentor, or Coach Faith Development?

In my earliest years of helping sportspeople develop their faith, I used a teaching approach. Having gone to schools in the USA, and having been raised in a Baptist church, teaching was the primary and only available model for intellectual and spiritual development. I started with the swimmers who attended the Sunday School class I was teaching in the late 1980s and early 1990s.

Many years later, after having succeeded a little and failed a lot, people began to seek me out for wisdom and for mentoring. They seem to value my experience and expertise, though I largely discount it. We sit and chat over coffee; I listen, tell stories, and offer options for their growth.

Most recently, I have begun coaching people who are seeking to develop their faith and those pursuing their calling to ministry. In this mode, I ask questions to help this person discover how he or she can pursue a call from God, develop a ministry, or simply be a more effective follower of Christ.

In developing the faith of sportspeople: Some people teach faith development. Other people mentor faith development. Still other people coach faith development. Which do you do? One, two, maybe all three? How are they different? What are the advantages of each? What are the liabilities of each?

Teaching faith development

When we teach faith development, we take an academic approach to training. It's about the delivery and processing of information. We assign books to read, make presentations, deliver lectures, and otherwise aim to improve the trainee's knowledge of the subject. The focus is usually on principles and practices. It may include research, writing papers, or making presentations to demonstrate the knowledge gained by the trainee. Teaching of Sports Chaplaincy happens at universities, in seminary classrooms, in sports ministries' meeting rooms, and via virtual learning platforms.

If you teach faith development, teach it effectively. Go for depth of understanding. Train minds and hearts to serve wisely. We need you to help the sports chaplaincy community be a healthy, intelligent, and well-integrated form of ministry.

Mentoring faith development

We who mentor people in the development of their faith do so with an eye toward continuing personal and professional development with our mentee(s). Most often, the mentorship takes place on an individual basis, rather than with a group. It can be delivered in person or via electronic media. Mentors in faith development provide a broad view, lending perspective across a career.

Mentors are less involved in the teaching or coaching of techniques, methods, or strategies than they are in sharing their insights, experiences, and expertise. This often leads to telling stories, asking challenging questions, and occasionally directly sharing wise counsel.

If you mentor sportspeople in the development of their faith, be sure to help your mentees gain perspective. Keep their overall wellbeing in mind. Help them develop their own vision, set goals, determine best practices, and lend wise counsel, as requested. Your mentees may gather great value by simply spending time in your altruistic presence.

Coaching faith development

We who coach faith development focus on the development of skills, and use questions (Socratic method) to help the trainee discover the why and how that shape their expressions of it.

We who coach the development of faith in sportspeople strive for understanding and processes that deliver excellent ministry. As we discuss ideas, options, strategies, and methods with trainees, we aim to help them apply the ideas to their local context, the community, the club or institution, the team, the coaching staff, and the competitors.

If you coach faith development as your method of training, do it with patience and thoughtfulness. Coaching takes time and intentional leadership. Coaching the development of faith in sportspeople will lead to depth of service, excellent ministry, and long-lasting results.

If you choose the coaching path, I highly recommend this book. Coaching 101 - Discover the Power of Coaching by Robert E. Logan and Sherilyn Carlton, with Tara Miller. sales@resourcezone.com.au

In developing the faith of sportspeople:

- Some people teach faith development. If that's you, teach it excellently.
- Other people mentor faith development. If that's you, share your experience and expertise freely.
- Still other people coach faith development. If that's you, ask skillful questions.
- You may even have opportunities to do all three. Focus on those hungry to learn, to grow, and to develop.

Faith Development Exercises for Elite Sportspeople

Since 1980 I have been engaged in the process of making disciples and since 1985, I have been using the same approach to this process. I learned it from my mentor, Fred Bishop of No Greater Love Ministries. This approach is very simple but allows for tremendous depth and flexibility for both the faith development leader and the disciple.

Having now served people in the sporting world since 1994, and continuing to make disciples along the way, this approach has proven to be quite effective. Please consider using this model or modifying it to suit your purposes. It can be used in one-to-one settings, with small groups, or even large groups.

If you are an elite level person of sport, I believe this process and its exercises will serve you well. Please look through the diagrams and descriptions of the processes to choose a point for beginning. As your faith develops, simply work your way around the four points of the cross to develop your faith completely. These exercises can help you continually grow across your lifetime, in sport and beyond it.

If you are someone serving the men and women of the elite sporting world, I believe this

FAITH DEVELOPMENT PROCESSES & RESOURCES

WHERE SHALL WE START?

process and its exercises can be of great value to you. This model can provide a simple framework upon which you can add your own favorite exercises and resources for making disciples of Christ Jesus. Simply use this model as a starting point and systematically aid the sportspeople in the development of their faith.

The process I use is pictured here. It focuses on four areas of development of Christian life. **Prayer – Study – Christian Community – Sharing One's Faith.** With sportspeople, I often call these exercises or drills that we practice developing our lives in Christ. I will explain, demonstrate, and assign a process or a resource for exercising, and in succeeding sessions we will review their discoveries, insights, and answer their questions. I always emphasize that Christian discipleship is a life-long process of growth and development.

To begin the development of one's faith I simply show the prospective disciple the diagram, explain that one's life in Christ is developed through a vertical relationship with God in prayer and study, as well as horizontal relationships with other believers (Christian community) and with people yet to believe (the sharing of one's faith). The stronger one's relationship with God grows, the shadow cast among the people surrounding him or her will be stronger and broader. Then I ask them, "Where would you like to start?" This question allows the disciple to indicate his or her greatest interest up front, leading to a greater likelihood of success and long-term development.

I believe hunger is the coin of the realm for the Kingdom of God. If a person is hungry to learn and grow, he or she will commit to your process. If the person is not genuinely hungry, it won't matter much what you do. *A sated man loathes honey, But to a famished man any bitter thing is sweet.* Proverbs 27:7 (NASB) Listen for their expression of hunger and feed exactly that. If you listen closely, they'll tell you where they itch. Scratch that.

Once the starting point is determined (almost always Prayer or Study), I flip the page over and begin to share processes and resources that facilitate our growth. Once we have delved into that first element, and learned its processes, we can choose another point in the diagram, and begin its development. I have found it best to ask the disciple each time, "Where should we go next?"

FAITH DEVELOPMENT PROCESSES & RESOURCES

PRAYER
PROCESSES
Adoration, Confession, Thanksgiving, Supplication
RESOURCES
The Competitor's Book of Prayer
SCRIPTURE
Philippians 4:6-8
Matthew 6:9-13

SHARING ONE'S FAITH
PROCESSES
Testimony (When, Where, Why?)
RESOURCES
The Four (FCA)
Four Spiritual Laws (AIA)
Roman Road
Bridge Illustration (Navigators)
SCRIPTURE
Philemon 6
1 Peter 3:15

CHRISTIAN COMMUNITY
PROCESSES
Jesus, 3, 12, 70, 120, 3,000, 5,000
RESOURCES
Family
Church
Groups
SCRIPTURE
Hebrews 10:23-25
Acts 2:42-47
Ephesians 4:1-7

STUDY
PROCESSES
Read, Study, Memorize, Meditate
RESOURCES
Devotionals
Study Bibles
Commentaries
Books
SCRIPTURE
2 Timothy 3:16
Hebrew 4:12

It's also wise to determine the duration of your discipleship process together. You can determine to meet for a set number of sessions, weeks, or months. To not set a timeline often leads to a sense of dread and failure if the frequency of meetings declines or circumstances cause you to stop meeting. Set the duration, complete those sessions, then determine if you should keep meeting or if it's time to move on.

Obviously, if there are resources you prefer or processes you like better, substitute them. These have been most helpful to me and to those I have trained.

Let's make disciples. This is my process, as adapted from a mentor. If you don't have a process, this one is better. Choose one and get after it.

Prayer

During the summer of 2014, my wife and I were at an airport on the way to New Orleans, Louisiana (USA) for vacation. As we sat at the airport, I was thinking about how we encourage competitors, athletes, and coaches, to pray about their lives in sport, but we seldom give them any good models for such prayer. I was grieved by the situation and thought someone should

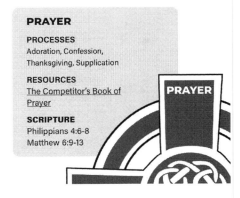

PRAYER

PROCESSES
Adoration, Confession, Thanksgiving, Supplication

RESOURCES
The Competitor's Book of Prayer

SCRIPTURE
Philippians 4:6-8
Matthew 6:9-13

do something about it. Since I was the one thinking about it, I determined I would give it a shot. I further thought, "Jesus gave his disciples a model, why should we not?" While at the airport that day I wrote about sixty situations in a sportsperson's life when it would be most helpful to know how to pray. That began a process of contemplation, prayer, writing prayers in my phone, testing them with competitors via text message and on my blog, and through discussions with sports ministry colleagues, pastors, and friends. That moment of contemplation began a nine-month process of writing prayers in my phone, and it resulted in the book, The Competitor's Book of Prayer. (ISBN – 1938254481)

In developing the life of prayer with sportspeople, I do as my mentor taught me and focus on four simple exercises of prayer – **Adoration** (prayers of worship and praise), **Confession** (prayers of agreement with God about matters of sin, righteousness, ability, or lack of it), **Thanksgiving** (expressions of thankfulness for what God has done), and **Supplication** (prayers of petition, asking God for provision or intercession for others).

Adoration – To express worship and praise to God for who He is. A few simple exercises for developing this form of prayer are these:

- A to Z worship. Simply wander through the alphabet thinking of words beginning with each letter descriptive of God's nature and attributes. For example, "Lord, you are Amazing, Benevolent, Compassionate, Dynamic, Exciting, Faithful, etc.…." This simple exercise grows one's understanding of the nature of God, and if one works at it, it can grow one's vocabulary as well. Praying this process out loud is even more powerful.

- Praying the Psalms. The Psalms are the Bible's prayer book and were written to be read or recited aloud. Choosing one or two for a period of prayer and reading them out loud is a dynamic part of adoration prayer.
- Singing one's favorite hymns or worship songs. Worship music has a powerful way of helping our souls to enter the presence of God and prepares our hearts for the other elements of a complete life of prayer.

Confession – To confess is to agree with God on a matter. Here are a couple of simple confession exercises:

- Agree with God about your sin and need for cleansing of your mind, soul, and conscience.
- For a deep, penetrating, and transforming exercise, consider this outline for repentance - https://riverofhopeministries.org/2018/02/11/breaking-up-the-fallow-ground-an-outline-for-repentance
- Agree with God about His goodness, grace, and provision. ("Lord, You are loving and gracious… You have all I need….")

Thanksgiving – To thank God for what He has done. Here is a simple thanksgiving exercise:

- Make a list of people, events, and things for which you're thankful. (Family, team, games, situations, accomplishments, etc.)

Supplication - To ask God to do something for someone. Below are a couple of simple supplication exercises:

- Make a list of people or situations for which you will pray today.
- Assign a day of each week to pray for different people, groups, or situations. For example:
  - ➤ Sunday – worship

- Monday – leaders of governments
- Tuesday – coaches and teammates
- Wednesday – family
- Thursday – career and personal needs
- Friday – friends and acquaintances
- Saturday – confession

Resources –

- Prayer in Sport - https://prayerinsport.blogspot.com/
- The (Online) Book of Common Prayer - https://bcponline.org/

Study

After a young lady's career as an elite level pole vaulter (athletics) had ended, and just prior to her beginning her study in the university's physician assistant program, she asked if I would meet with her weekly over coffee to help develop her faith. I agreed and during our first meeting together I shared my simple faith development diagram and asked her, "Where would you like to start?" She said, "I don't really know how to read my Bible." I said, "I think I can help you." I

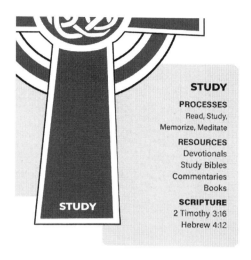

STUDY

PROCESSES
Read, Study,
Memorize, Meditate

RESOURCES
Devotionals
Study Bibles
Commentaries
Books

SCRIPTURE
2 Timothy 3:16
Hebrew 4:12

bought her a One Year Bible to facilitate her devotional reading, and we met weekly for the next year. Along the way I shared the Study exercises found below and watched her understanding of and her love for the scripture grow exponentially. I was thrilled to see her complete her course of academic study, to participate in her wedding ceremony, and to see her thrive in her career, as well as become a mother.

In prayer we express our hearts to God, in study we listen to His counsel, His comfort, His expressions of love and compassion. I have found it most productive for developing faith in sportspeople to help them learn a few simple principles and exercises.

Study - a few principles and exercises follow.

- **Read, Study, Memorize, Meditate.**

  ➤ To read is to simply take in the information. This is most often simple, daily devotional reading of the Bible.

  ➤ To study is to ask probing questions of the text being studied, to consider and to perceive the meaning of the scripture.

➤ To memorize is to commit the chosen text and its reference to one's memory to arm one's soul for thinking God's thoughts after Him.

➤ To meditate is to think deeply about the truth of scripture, to consider the implications of the truth, and to make application of the truth to one's convictions, lifestyle, and relationships.

- **Architecture of the Bible.** Few people come to the Bible with an understanding of how it is constructed. Many expect it to read like most books of western literature, to flow chronologically from event to event. The Bible is not like this at all, rather it is arranged by types of literature as follows:

  ➤ **Old Testament** (39 books)
    - Law (5 books)
    - History (12 books)
    - Poetry (5 books)
    - Major Prophets (5 books)
    - Minor Prophets (12 books)

  ➤ **New Testament** (27 books)
    - Gospels (4 books)
    - History (1 book)
    - Pauline Epistles (13 books)
    - General Epistles (8 books)
    - Apocalyptic Literature (1 book)

  Understanding this arrangement of the forms of Bible literature and the various ways to interpret them is most helpful in grasping the truth of scripture.

- **Inductive Bible Study Method.** The development of this skill is transformative to the growth of one's faith. The grasp of it can help the follower of Christ to discern the truth of the Bible and to apply it to life.

➤ **Observation** – in this step of the method, one simply reads the scripture and asks observational questions of it. Questions like: who, where, when, and how? Seeking answers to these questions assist the reader in seeing matters in the text, its characters and narrative more clearly.

➤ **Interpretation** – in this step of the method, one asks questions to discern the meaning of the scripture. Questions like: Why would He say this? What does this mean? What is the big idea? Why is this important? These questions clarify meaning and purpose.

➤ **Correlation** – after having observed clearly and interpreted the meaning of the scripture, we are wise to take time to check our perceptions against other sources of truth. Are there other places in the Bible speaking of this same issue or event? Are there commentaries or other resources we should consult to enlighten our understanding?

➤ **Application** – after observing the text, interpreting its meaning, and correlating our interpretations wisely, it is time to apply the truth of scripture to life. Asking questions like these are helpful to this step in the process: What does this truth demand of me? If this is true, what does God want me to do about it? Given I am understanding God's will in this text, so what? How can I apply this truth to my daily life?

• **Resources**
   ➤ The Bible Project - https://bibleproject.com/
   ➤ YouVersion Bible app - https://www.youversion.com/
   ➤ Bible Gateway - https://www.biblegateway.com/
   ➤ Heart of a Champion – https://www.crosstrainingpublishing.com/shop/heart-of-a-champion

To read, study, memorize, and meditate on the Bible accomplishes the process described in Psalm 119:130, ***The unfolding of Your words gives light; It gives understanding to the simple.*** (NASB)

Christian Community

In my first months of serving a college football staff and team, I saw how terribly isolated and devoid of Christian community were the lives of the coaches and players. Because of the incredibly consuming nature of their work, their world shrinks down to the one hundred plus people making up the team, coaches, and support staff. They seldom know who they can trust outside that circle, and that includes the men and women of the Church.

CHRISTIAN COMMUNITY

CHRISTIAN COMMUNITY

PROCESSES
Jesus, 3, 12, 70, 120, 3,000, 5,000

RESOURCES
Family
Church
Groups

SCRIPTURE
Hebrews 10:23-25
Acts 2:42-47
Ephesians 4:1-7

STUDY

When I saw this playing out in the life of the head coach I wondered, "Who cares for this man's soul?" Most people are thrilled to be around him when we're winning, but if things are not going so well, they quickly disappear. I knew I needed to build a group of men to surround him with no strings attached. He needed a group of loyal, caring, and consistent brothers to walk along with him. None of us would ask him for sideline passes, free tickets, team gear, autographs, or to shoot selfies on our phones. We loved him as Christ loves us (John 13:34-35).

We built that group, and across almost thirty years, long after the coach had moved onto other opportunities, after more than a dozen other men have participated in the group and moved on, a couple of us are still meeting weekly for Christian community.

The people of sport live in a complex network of relationships and experience community in ways that are both wonderfully rich and uplifting as well as corrupt and demeaning. Sportspeople relate daily with their teammates, with opponents, with coaches, with officials, trainers, office staff, equipment managers, and even with the elements of the sport itself.

Like any community, the sport world is either enriched or impoverished by the people who populate it. The media seem obsessed with reporting the stories of those in sport that have corrupted it by means of cheating, lying, abusing drugs, or engaging in foolish sexual behavior. This is what the spectators see of the sport community. What those outside the sport world fail to see is the rich depth of relationships which are forged in the fires of intense competition, long hours spent together, in the exultation of winning and the grief of losing.

The Holy Scriptures eloquently describe the nature of true Christian community in both narrative passages like Acts chapter 2 and in didactic passages like Ephesians chapter 4. If one is actively engaged in sport, he or she can see the faces and hear the voices of teammates when reading the verses below from Ephesians 4:1-6. *Therefore I, the prisoner of the Lord, urge you to walk in a manner worthy of the calling with which you have been called, 2 with all humility and gentleness, with patience, bearing with one another in love, 3 being diligent to keep the unity of the Spirit in the bond of peace. 4 There is one body and one Spirit, just as you also were called in one hope of your calling; 5 one Lord, one faith, one baptism, 6 one God and Father of all who is over all and through all and in all.* (NASB)

This dynamic exhortation from the Apostle Paul applies both to the Church as well as to any sports team. If a team were to exercise love, and would diligently maintain unity with humility and gentleness, the team would surely experience a profound sense of community. This would be true for those who have yet to commit themselves to Christ, but it would certainly be more likely to occur and more powerfully energized if they were filled with the Holy Spirit as believers are.

Sport, like other experiences of community, includes relationships with saints and sinners. It exists in a complicated web of relationships with teammates, opponents, officials, coaches, and even the competitor's relationship with the sport itself. Such community is a powerful experience in the life of the follower of Christ. The Christian sportsperson is informed by the Scripture and energized by the Holy

Spirit. Sport is an experience of community.

Finding a local church with which to connect is a constant challenge for elite sportspeople. Often their lifestyles require frequent moves from city to city, uprooting their families, and fracturing only recently formed bonds of friendship. In addition to these issues, the higher profile sportspeople feel even more marginalized in this process. They wonder if the congregation will love and respect them as anyone else, or if their celebrity status will compromise their hopes to find a genuine, loving, and nurturing community of faith.

Your role in this process is most crucial to the elite sportsperson's experience with the local church. Your first thought may be to simply take him or her along with you. That may even be the best option. I would suggest one particular question to ask of the one expressing interest in finding a church. "What sort of a church are you looking for?" Your friend is then free to describe his or her primary thoughts about the ideal church. He or she may mention a denomination, a worship style, or a theological emphasis. If you're well informed about the churches in your community, you can point your friend to one or a few you believe could be a good fit. You could certainly offer to escort your friend to a church and make introductions to the church leaders and other parishioners of your acquaintance.

Christian Community Exercise

COMMUNITY AND COMMITMENT

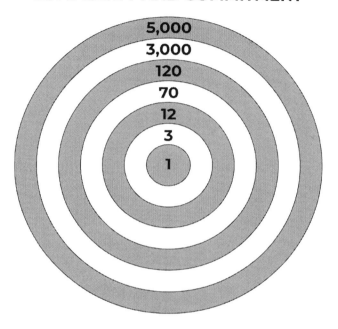

This chart diagrams different sets of people and how deeply they were committed to Jesus and His purposes.

- 5,000 – In Mark 6:34-44, Jesus feeds 5,000 men (plus women and children) with 5 loaves of bread and 2 fish. Their level of commitment was to listen and eat lunch.
- 3,000 – In Acts 2:41, we read that 3,000 people received Christ on the Day of Pentecost. Their level of commitment was to trust Christ for salvation.
- 120 – Earlier that same day there were 120 Disciples of Christ praying in an upper room. Their level of commitment involved prayer and waiting for the Lord's promise.
- 70 – In Luke 10:1, we see that Jesus sent out 70 people in pairs as laborers

in the harvest He was to reap in the souls of people. Their commitment included taking greater risks and sharing Christ's message with others around Judea.

- 12 – Jesus had 12 disciples who traveled with Him for the three years of his ministry on earth. Their commitment meant leaving their careers and eventually losing their lives in His service.
- 3 – Peter, James, and John were the only three disciples present at the Mount of Transfiguration and went further into the Garden of Gethsemane than the other disciples. Their commitment is seen in the leadership roles they assume later in their lives.
- 1 – Jesus was the only one of these to die for all the others. His commitment is supreme.

Think through these concentric circles and their respective levels of commitment.

- ➤ Who is most committed to you and your values? List the names of three.
- ➤ Who would be the twelve people who have a significant commitment to you and your life in sport? List their names.
- ➤ What groups have similar commitments to yours at levels seventy and one hundred twenty? Write down the name of those groups.
- ➤ With what groups do you rub shoulders in your life but don't have similar depth of commitment? List those groups at the three thousand and five thousand levels.

Given all that you've observed in the diagram and scriptures, with whom does it seem Jesus spent the most and highest quality time? (Obviously, those in the smallest circles, and He spent less time with those in wider circles.) Working through this diagram with the elite sportsperson can help him or her to identify groups, crowds, and individuals as they relate to the sportsperson. The process of writing in names of persons and groups can be very helpful in drawing healthy boundaries and leaning into their most reliable relationships and communities.

Sharing One's Faith

In the mid-1990s, I was serving a college (American) football team, and one of the players with whom I had developed a strong relationship was a senior punter from the Memphis, Tennessee area. We had occasionally talked about spiritual things, I had given him a New Testament to read, but we were approaching the end of his career and thus the end of my opportunities to see him regularly. I invited him to meet me for pizza one day as I wanted to speak with him most clearly and directly about his need for a relationship with Christ Jesus.

SHARING ONE'S FAITH
PROCESSES
Testimony (When, Where, Why?)

RESOURCES
The Four (FCA)
Four Spiritual Laws (AIA)
Roman Road
Bridge Illustration
(Navigators)

SCRIPTURE
Philemon 6
1 Peter 3:15

SHARING ONE'S FAITH

He and I met at the restaurant, ordered our lunch, and he beat me to the punch by saying, "You know, Mr. Roger, I have been thinking about why I started playing football in high school, why I came to SIU, why I started coming to chapel, and why we became friends. I think it was so I could know the Lord." I said, "Yeah, that could be. Let's talk more about that." As we chatted over some Quatro's deep pan pizza, we discussed the truth of the gospel, his trust in Christ, and how to grow his relationship with God. That was a great day, and now he is a faithful husband, father, and pilot for Federal Express.

Learning how to share one's faith in a clear, concise manner is a valuable tool in the development of a sportsperson's life. Two scriptures in particular shape my approach to this portion of faith development, and two exercises are most helpful to its implementation.

I believe I Peter 3:15 outlines the most appropriate approach to sharing one's faith in the sporting community. It reads, ***But in your hearts revere Christ as Lord. Always be prepared to give an answer to everyone who asks you to give the reason for the hope that you have. But do this with gentleness and respect,*** (NIV)

In addition, Philemon verse 6 helps the growing follower of Christ to grasp one of the effects of sharing one's faith. It reads, ***and I pray that the sharing of your faith may promote the knowledge of all the good that is ours in Christ.*** (RSV)

Faith sharing Exercises

Sharing Your Story – the beauty of sharing your story is that it is beyond argument. You're simply sharing your story. The weakness of it is that it's your story. Not everyone is or can be in the same situation. Your story begins and ends with you. Here is a very effective exercise for sharing your faith story:

- When, where, and why?

  Answer these three questions in the most simple and brief way possible:
  - ➤ When did you commit your life to Christ Jesus?
  - ➤ Where were you when you committed your life to Christ?
  - ➤ Why did you decide to commit your life to Jesus?
  - ➤ Try to answer these questions in the form of a brief story.

Sharing Jesus' Story – there are numerous ways to share the gospel (good news) of Christ Jesus with others. The beauty of sharing Jesus' story is that it begins and ends with Him. The person one shares it with must deal with Jesus. This is not about the person sharing His story. There is plenty of room for one to choose an expression for sharing Jesus' story best fitting his or her personality and communication style. The following are but four of the ways to share one's faith most prominently used by sportspeople to share Jesus' story:

- **That's Good News!** - https://www.inviteresources.com/store/good-news-epub#add-cart-form
- **The Four Spiritual Laws by Athletes in Action** (a division of Cru) - https://www.cru.org/us/en/how-to-know-god/would-you-like-to-know-god-personally.html
- **The Four by Fellowship of Christian Athletes** - https://thefour.fca.org/
- **The Bridge to Life by Navigators** – https://www.navigators.org/resource/the-bridge-to-life/

Regardless of which form you choose for sharing Jesus' story, the gospel, be sure to include these elements:

- The love of God
- The fact and consequences of our rebellion toward God.
- The necessity of confession of and repentance from sin.
- The trust of Jesus' sacrificial death and triumphant resurrection.
- The commitment and the confession aloud of one's life to Christ.

Points of Emphasis for Professional Sport

As outlined by Walt Enoch.

Prayer

- Prayer points of emphasis –
  - ➤ Prayer is modeled in the Bible study.
  - ➤ Prayer is offered by the chaplain and players at team chapels.
  - ➤ Prayer takes place in a prayer circle at the conclusion of chapel.
  - ➤ Prayer is done in the locker room before taking the field.
  - ➤ Prayers are said on the sideline with players as they request it.

Study

- Bible study points of emphasis – "Teaching the Scripture has always been what I have stuck to and has kept the men coming over the years. I cannot emphasize that enough."
  - ➤ Weekly meetings are best.
  - ➤ Coaches Study
  - ➤ Players Study
  - ➤ Couples Study
  - ➤ Game Day Chapel
  - ➤ Verse by verse studies work very well. Walt's Tuesday study, which he led for over thirty years, walked through the entire Bible several times.

➤ Walt used inductive Bible study method and developed his own study guides.

➤ Emphasize Matthew, Mark, Luke John, Acts and Romans.

➤ Allow the group studies to prompt opportunities for individual meetings with players or coaches.

Challenge

If your ministry role has you serving elite level, professional, high-profile competitors or the coaches who lead them, you are in a unique position. You are among a select few people who will be allowed into their circle of friends, teammates, and colleagues. Yours is a place of remarkable privilege and immense responsibility.

Further, if this person has shown interest in growing his or her relationship with Christ Jesus, you are given a tremendous opportunity. As you step into this unique and transformational role, may I remind you of these simple points of emphasis?

- Respect their time constraints.
- Embrace their sport's culture.
- Communicate directly.
- Demonstrate genuine interest in them.
- Invite them into your home.
- Love extravagantly.
- Serve selflessly.

FAITH DEVELOPMENT PROCESSES & RESOURCES

WHERE SHALL WE START?

Keep your approach to the faith development of those in your charge simple and clear. Help them build a strong, enduring, dynamic relationship with Christ Jesus through prayer and study. Help them to also build relationships with other believers, as well as with those yet to believe.

As we walk with these people of sport, the ripple effects of our service with them have an incalculable impact across years, decades, and lifetimes. Our service will be most evident in how they compete, how they live as spouses and parents, and how they share their faith with others.

Roger D. Lipe

Psalm 90:12-17

About the author –

Roger Lipe is the Character Coach Director for Nations of Coaches, a ministry to college basketball in the USA. He also serves as character coach to Men's Basketball at Southern Illinois University.

Roger served with the Fellowship of Christian Athletes in southern Illinois for twenty-seven years. He was born and raised in Carbondale, Illinois (USA) and currently resides there with his wife, Sharon. Their son Jason, his wife Jenn, and granddaughters Addison and Elise are treasures to his soul.

Roger is the author of fifteen books for ministry in sport. His global network of friends and colleagues has enabled him to make dozens of international trips to over twenty nations on six continents to facilitate the growth of sports chaplaincy. He is a member of the Global Leadership Team for the Global Sports Chaplaincy Association.

Other publications by Roger D. Lipe –

Front Lines - Becoming an Effective Sports Chaplain or Character Coach - ISBN-10 1952222028

Heart of a Champion – Devotions for the People of Sport - ISBN-10 1929478704

Free to Compete – Reflections on Sport from a Christian Perspective - ISBN-10 1938254155

The Competitor's Book of Prayer - ISBN-10 1938254481

Whistles and Wedding Rings - Devotions for Coaches and Spouses – ISBN-10 9781938254703

Coaching: Our Family Business - Devotions for Coaches and Spouses - ISBN-10 1938254996

Transforming Lives in Sport - ISBN 1-929478-75-5

Made in the USA
Monee, IL
20 July 2023

39179102R00033